SAVED 365

BIBLE PRINCIPLES FOR YOUR BEST LIFE

CHRIS HARRIS

WESTBOW
PRESS®
A DIVISION OF THOMAS NELSON
& ZONDERVAN

WestBow Press books may be ordered through booksellers or by contacting:

WestBow Press
A Division of Thomas Nelson & Zondervan
1663 Liberty Drive
Bloomington, IN 47403
www.westbowpress.com
844-714-3454

Because of the dynamic nature of the Internet, any web addresses or links contained in this book may have changed since publication and may no longer be valid. The views expressed in this work are solely those of the author and do not necessarily reflect the views of the publisher, and the publisher hereby disclaims any responsibility for them.

Any people depicted in stock imagery provided by Getty Images are models, and such images are being used for illustrative purposes only. Certain stock imagery © Getty Images.

Risen King Productions L.L.C.

Unless otherwise indicated, all Scripture quotations are taken from King James version of the Bible, public domain.

Scriptures marked NIV are taken from THE HOLY BIBLE, NEW INTERNATIONAL VERSION®, NIV® Copyright © 1973, 1978, 1984, 2011 by Biblica, Inc.® Used by permission. All rights reserved worldwide.

Scripture quotations marked NLT are taken from the Holy Bible, New Living Translation, copyright © 1996, 2004, 2015 by Tyndale House Foundation. Used by permission of Tyndale House Publishers, Inc., Carol Stream, Illinois 60188. All rights reserved.

Scriptures marked NASB are taken from the NEW AMERICAN STANDARD BIBLE®, Copyright © 1960, 1962, 1963, 1968, 1971, 1972, 1973, 1975, 1977, 1995 by The Lockman Foundation. Used by permission.

Scripture marked (AMP) are taken from the Amplified Bible, Copyright © 2015 by The Lockman Foundation, La Habra, CA 90631. All rights reserved.

ISBN: 979-8-3850-0263-4 (sc)
ISBN: 979-8-3850-0262-7 (e)

Print information available on the last page.

WestBow Press rev. date: 2/16/2024

CONTENTS

INTRO

You can read this book in less than a day and improve the rest of your life. God intends for every human to live an outstanding life. He is standing by, almost pleading, to offer all the assistance we'll ever need to be victorious in every situation we'll ever encounter.

The Holy Spirit is a teacher (1 Cor 2:13, Luke 12:12). The Holy Spirit filled my education with valuable nuggets the first year after I received it. Those nuggets improved my life and mindset and could have prevented many headaches and problems in the years leading up to that. It revealed simple key pieces of wisdom which improved my interactions, relationships, and behavior. The more I learned, the more I realized God truly has an answer for everything from parenting, health, paying bills, and everything in between.

I've sat in Bible class many times and thought, *If I had only known this earlier…* This book is a condensed summary of hundreds of hours of learning to make universal truths readily available to anyone interested in a better life. Some of these include:

1. Not arguing with anyone
2. Being anxious about nothing
3. Not being afraid because fear is from the devil
4. Avoiding strife/following peace with everyone
5. All authority comes from God

I gained wisdom through (1) the Bible, (2) directly from the Holy Spirit, and (3) outstanding pastors and teachers.

The truths outlined in this book are Bible-based. This means if you reject or have issues with the Bible, you'll have a problem with these writings. However, if you strive to consistently put these truths to work in everyday life, you *will* have a better life. Through God your *best* life is possible.

01

DON'T GIVE PEARLS TO SWINE

Hebrews 11:6 says, logically, that he who comes to God must first believe that he is. Psalm 14:1 says (to paraphrase), that a fool can look at trees, beautiful flowers, the sky, sun, human body, reproduction, science, and the complex systems working together to reproduce and sustain life and still say, "There is no God."

Jesus said in Matthew 7:6, "Give not that which is holy unto the dogs, neither cast ye your pearls before swine." Those who have sincerely studied, tested and practiced Bible principles with diligence know it's the word of God—the same force that created humans, the earth, and everything in it. Some say they believe humans, the earth, science, etc. are just coincidence. If you fall into this category, this book is not for you.

In 2 Timothy 2:2, it says to teach knowledge and truth to *faithful* men. Faith refers to a strong belief in something you can't see or fully explain. This book is for the faithful. It's designed to release regenerative power that will perpetually elevate you, who puts it into practice, to higher levels than ever before.

02

HAVE YOU OPENED YOUR GIFT?

It's hard for the human mind to comprehend that God and his word are one and the same. You can't separate the two because the only thing God can't do is lie. If he says something that isn't true, he wouldn't be God. He's too powerful to lie. Many view the Bible—God's written word—as a list of rules and restrictions. This is a common misconception. The truth is, it's God's will and testament with instructions on how to activate things we have available through Jesus Christ. When many (often rich) people die, they often leave wills with conditions attached to them. Recipients don't generally avoid a will altogether or refuse to do what it says for them to do to receive the benefits.

The Bible contains valuable benefits and promises with directions on how to put them in action. Few people living at the time Jesus was alive—or today—realize the gravity of what he did and made available. Those born after Jesus died and rose from the dead are in a far better position than before.

One reason is they received gifts.

Ephesians 4:8 says that after Jesus rose from the dead and went back to heaven, he gave gifts to men ("men" includes women). When the one who made the world and everything in it hands out gifts, it's something to take notice and take advantage of. But most people don't—like someone whose rich uncle left them a big inheritance they don't even know about; or someone with a million dollars in the bank without an ATM card or a way to get it out. It's like a big beautifully wrapped Christmas gift that got misplaced or left under the tree because the recipient never came or bothered to pick it up.

03

TERRIFIC BUNDLE, UNBEATABLE PRICE (BEING A "KNOW-IT-ALL" IN CHRIST)

I always thought of the Holy Spirit as something that would be a burden growing up, one that would weigh me down and limit me. So, I avoided it for years because of fear and reluctance to take on the responsibility. When I finally received it, went to Bible class, and studied at home, I learned my old way of thinking deceived me. A million dollars, believe it or not, is a lot of responsibility if someone gives it to you. That doesn't mean you should turn it down. Who would choose to continue living in a shack because they don't want the responsibility of keeping up a big house? Not many! But for years, I, like many others, settled for an inferior life. I had heard, but hadn't let it sink in, that the Holy Spirit was a valuable asset sent to help.

The price of the Holy Spirit is very high. Fortunately for us, Jesus paid the full price on the cross already. The only cost to you and me is our self-will, which, if we're completely honest with ourselves, hasn't been that great and caused more than a few problems. Another comparison to not accepting Jesus would be if somebody left you a 50-yard line ticket to the super bowl, wrote you explaining how and where to pick it up, gave you transportation to get there, but you never bothered to act on it. After I received the Holy Spirit on September 14, 2007, and gave up my own will for his, I found out benefits are too many to list. More than a year later, I'm discovering new perks all the time, which I expect to continue for the rest of my life.

The Bible says those who receive the Holy Spirit receive "the fullness" of God (John 1:16 and Ephesians 3:19). Fullness includes the knowledge, nature, and power of God. The average person might be uncomfortable with this due to fear of what sounds like a tremendous responsibility. As a result, they might not accept and open the gift that's available to them.

God created the universe and knows all things. Therefore, if I have the fullness of God through his Holy Spirit, I have access to knowledge of all things. It excludes nothing that's helpful for me to know. Standing in the way of accessing that knowledge is sin, self-will, ignorance and not believing in God's word.

Saved people don't know everything immediately, it would overwhelm their brain. But the Holy Spirit, besides being a teacher, brings information to an individual's remembrance at all appropriate times (John 14:26). That's why it says when they bring you before judges and authorities, don't worry about how to defend yourself or what you'll say (Luke 12:11). Because, in that hour, what you will say will be *given* to you (Matthew 10:19) – it is a gift!

PEACE

Several years ago, I worked for a government agency. The sneakiness, plotting, and backbiting there were tremendous. There were several employees who had been there many years and were knowledgeable about ways to entrap others, get them in trouble, or generally make their co-workers' lives miserable. I was not very good at being sneaky and plotting against people, but I tried to imitate those who were to an extent. After all, they survived and did well for many years in the same environment I wanted to be successful in. They made decent salaries and seemed to have pleasant lives. They were already at the point where I was trying to get. Therefore, it was logical to watch them and try to be like them to some degree. But for people in God's kingdom, this should never be the case.

Operating in the kingdom involves thinking and acting on a higher level that often doesn't make sense to the human mind. I didn't realize those I imitated weren't truly happy, and as long as I tried functioning like unsaved people, there was no peace in my life. I was constantly worried and on edge. By comparison, after I accepted God, I maintained almost constant peace, no matter what was going on around me.

Shortly after I'd accepted Jesus as my savior and received the Holy Spirit in 2007, I applied for a management role. I was clearly the most qualified, but it went to another applicant. I was disappointed. Previously, losing the promotion would've upset and made me angry about injustice. I would have stressed over it and spent hours thinking about what to do next. But after joining the kingdom and understanding how it works through the Bible, I knew I didn't have to be angry, worry, or seek my own justice.

Romans 8:28 applied to the situation, saying "all things work together for good for those that love the Lord." I loved the Lord, therefore getting passed over for the job was good. The human mind asks, "How can it be good to be passed over for a better position making more money?" Instead of dwelling on stressful things that could frustrate me, waste time, and make me unhappy, I learned to dwell on passages of the Bible that applied to my situation. I sleep great at night; many millionaires can't say that. So, though I was disappointed, I thanked God, knowing the job wasn't for me. A year later, the economy took a turn, the agency's budget was cut, and they eliminated the supervisor role I'd applied for. Being passed over turned out to be a blessing. I would've had a pay raise for a few months, then been without a job in a climate where jobs were scarce.

I've found tremendous peace and reassurance knowing that promotion comes from God. In this case, it became easy to see why not getting the job was actually good. This built up my faith tremendously. However, I realize I won't always know the reason(s) God allows a thing to happen. But my faith in God's word comforts and reassures me that *all* things are working for my good, regardless of how it looks or whether I understand it or not. What an awesome feeling! Because his word says it, that's enough.

Because of the budget cuts, many co-workers were nervous about their job and the possibility of not meeting financial obligations, such as car payments, kids' tuition, etc. I didn't share their anxiety because I knew Philippians 4:19 says God will supply all my needs, not according to the economy, or budget of my employer, but "according to his riches in glory…" (Philippians 4:19).

Once I accepted Christ and took time to know and understand what the Bible said, I left the world's system. God became responsible for me. He's not dependent on shaky factors like the stock market, fluctuating budgets, political changes, taxes, etc. He can and will provide for me through my current employment, or other ways.

Bishop William Reynolds in Columbus, Ohio, once taught a sermon entitled, "Are You More Than a Bird?" in which he emphasized birds don't work, worry about what they'll eat, where they'll live, health insurance, what they'll wear, etc., yet they look great, have plenty to eat, and have everything they need. They get up in the morning and fulfill their purpose, which is to sing—a form of worshipping God. They seem to know everything they need is taken care of and was put in place before they were born.

They have beautiful feathers and have plenty of building material to construct comfortable homes. Their food supply is everywhere. They have transportation (I recently read that a bird the size of a person's hand can travel from the Amazon Rain Forest in South America to Pennsylvania in about ten days). The bird's life is a beautifully simplistic illustration of God's love and how he operates.

Our heavenly father doesn't have problems with child support. Everything we'll ever need—food, oxygen, water, shelter, etc.—was put here well before we arrived. We get into trouble if we lose sight of that, start trusting ourselves, and seeking our own solutions to obtain what God has already made available. So, the difference between living with anxiety, fear, and stress versus God's peace is finding out who we are, knowing God's character, and how his kingdom operates. I tried things the Biblical way in various areas and subjects, and it's never let me down. In 1 Peter 2:9, it says God's people are peculiar people. They have different ways of thinking, reacting, and going about things.

The Bible is full of promises but hasn't let one person down in thousands of years. Because I know this and allowed God to come and take up residence inside of me to help me, I can live in a form of heaven while on Earth. Because most people haven't given their heart to God, it's easy to see why those in the kingdom can seem weird. For one thing, they have ability to maintain peace during hectic and unstable situations.

A co-worker once shared with me they could barely function due to worrying about their job and possible pay cuts. She became so stressed, playing out different scenarios in her mind, that she removed her name from a list where she had signed up to buy cookie dough for a fundraiser. I wished I could transplant everything I'd learned about God's richness and love into her mind so she could relax. Because I know about the riches, power, and love of my heavenly father, I don't have to be affected by negative forecasts about the weather, finances, terror threats, bird or swine flu, school shootings, etc. I know God provides everything I need. He came to live inside me to help, lead, guide and protect me from the minute I let him in. For the thirty-three years before that, he was just standing by, patiently waiting for me to invite him in.

When I don't rely on the Holy Spirit, my rational mind kicks in, which Jeremiah 17:9 says is "…the most deceitful of all things. It is incurable. No one can understand how deceitful it is." Our mind and its limited information can have us scared, tricked, stressed out, caught up in temptation, and sidetracked. In his wisdom and mercy, God recognized we are too weak and vulnerable on our own. What could be more priceless than complete calm when things around us seem completely chaotic?

One of the most well-known scriptures is Philippians 4:6, which says "The Lord is my shepherd, I shall not want…" It goes on to say, "He maketh me to lie down in green pastures." This language doesn't indicate a request or suggestion. Some people seem addicted to stress and constant activity. But in the kingdom of God, he requires some time for us to relax and be restored. One Biblical rule that impacted me is to be "careful," (meaning "anxious") about nothing (Philippians 4:6). So, not only did God say that we don't have to worry, he *commanded* us not to be anxious.

I shouldn't be afraid because I serve a God who said he would protect me and he has never lost a battle. He said he would provide for me and has never let anybody down. God is 100% faithful. If I worry, it means I'm afraid God won't do what he said he would, something that's never happened in the history of the universe! As a result, when I catch myself being anxious, I stop and say, "Wait a minute!" I identify what's going on and realize I don't have to be that way. In fact, I'm commanded not to be that way! I'm better than that and the God I serve is bigger than any real or perceived problem. God said he'd never leave or forsake me. If that's true, how could I be afraid? He said he'd work everything (not some things) out for my good—even when enemies try to destroy me. I can calm down, breathe a sigh of relief and say, "Thank you Lord!" Then I can sit back and watch him work in my favor. This is priceless!

Entertainer Michael Jackson had some of the greatest earning potential of anyone who ever lived. He could sell out any stadium in hours. But apparently, he couldn't lay down and sleep normally—something that costs nothing, yet is invaluable. Hebrews 4 says those that (1) believe in God and (2) stop sinning, enter God's rest. When you enter God's rest, you can prosper and feel good without any negative side effects.

GIFTS, GIFTS, MORE GIFTS

Galatians 5:22 identifies other benefits available through Christ and the Holy Spirit, including peace, joy, and temperance (the ability not to be emotionally up and down), to name a few. I have found tutor, memory aid, consoler, appetite suppressant, doctor, lawyer, GPS, parenting coach, mediator, financial planner, motivational speaker, confidence builder, thesaurus, security system, and friend, to also be included.

PRICE OF A GIFT

In Luke 11:13, Jesus asked his disciples, if evil parents give gifts to their children, "How much more will your heavenly Father give the Holy Spirit to those who ask him?" The Holy Spirit itself is a gift. It's not something you pursue to get. On the day of Pentecost, it fell on the people (Acts 11:15). Because it's a gift, you just receive it, open it up, and use it for its intended purpose, or it does you no good. Many times, you must refer to an owner's manual to put a gift to work in your life.

Romans 3:23 states, "All have sinned." Romans 6:23 says, "The wages of sin is death." The bad news: because Adam sinned, and we descended from Adam, we're born into inherited sin and death (separation from God, the source of life). The good news is that Christ died and shed innocent blood to pay for everything. As a result, we can stop what we're doing, give up our will, and join with Christ, an opportunity available to everyone.

One reason Jesus went back to heaven after being resurrected was so the comforter (Holy Spirit) could come. The Bible urges people to stop from their work. (Proverb 23:4). Hebrews 3:18 says those who believe can enter his rest. "His rest" includes the true peace and security of knowing the creator of the world will live inside you and help with all your problems, both present and future. All you have to do is, "Repent, and be baptized.…in the name of Jesus Christ for the remission of sins, and ye shall receive the gift of the Holy Ghost" (Acts 2:38). Some people neglect this because they don't want the perceived burden/responsibility, or they can't believe it's that simple. In actuality, it's not that simple, but we don't have to do the hard part. That's already taken care of - Jesus paid the death price/penalty on the cross.

As long as Jesus was with his disciples, they didn't need a comforter. Jesus comforted and helped them. Human spirits are pessimistic, selfish, and prideful. They hate to submit. It takes certain willpower and discipline for the human spirit to agree with and submit to the Holy Spirit, which is all-knowing and through whom nothing good is impossible. If we ask God, he will help us with discipline and willpower, which can be useful in all areas of our lives.

GIFT OF KNOWLEDGE-WHERE THE FISH ARE

"For to one is given by the Spirit the word of wisdom; to another, the word of knowledge by the same Spirit" (1 Corinthians 12:8).

Simon and some of Jesus's disciples, some who were professional fisherman, once fished all night long with no success. After returning to shore, Jesus instructed them to sail back into deep water and release the fishing nets again. "Cast the net on the right side of the ship and ye shall find" John 21:6. They were reluctant and probably tired. Despite how they felt, they did what Jesus instructed anyway and caught so many fish they had to have help from another boat to carry them. This is an example of the spiritual gift of knowledge. God likely didn't create new fish, but simply revealed where the fish were—they had been fishing in the wrong place. What they were looking for was surprisingly close. The word of knowledge from the Lord was all they needed to unlock the blessing he had already put in place with them in mind.

DOWNSIDE

Part of the reason I rejected the Holy Spirit for many years was that I thought I'd have to give up things I liked and enjoyed and become very restricted. But everything the world offered became dim by comparison after becoming saved. What I thought I'd miss out on was nothing but death and deception. I didn't smoke, but cigarettes are a good example. It says on the package that it might kill you. But people still pay to do it anyway. I had a rental property once. The tenant smoked heavily, despite being on oxygen. If someone takes a knife and cuts themselves, they could be given any number of diagnoses. People do other things that are just as harmful (ever watch anybody die of cancer or lung disease from smoking?), but because the harm doesn't show up immediately, it's accepted.

Romans 12:2 says not to be conformed—meaning shaped—by the things of "this world." This is great advice because, when you take a step back and look, the world is crazy on many levels. The world tells us to drink to cope with problems. Unfortunately, alcohol attacks the liver—an organ needed to live. A huge percentage of problems—broken marriages, legal troubles, fractured relationships etc.—can be traced back to alcohol. It can be expensive. Yet it remains one of the world's leading remedies.

As a young adult, I had financial challenges and was advised to record and keep track of all expenses. I discovered the percentage of my budget spent on alcohol was staggering. People routinely do things against their self-interest in many ways, often without realizing it. Romans 12:2 tells us to be "transformed," or changed. I've learned that change isn't a sudden process. Once one turns their life over to God, they progress in wisdom, knowledge, patience, self-control, and other areas continuously if they allow the Holy Spirit to do its work.

When I first got saved, I missed drinking. It was something I'd enjoyed and was used to doing, especially during sporting events. Then, one day I realized I didn't miss it anymore. Now when I picture a liquor bottle, I think of a headache. When I think of beer, I feel tired and bloated. Yet for many years, I drank in a destructive cycle. Sure, there were enjoyable times. But now I know I can have just as much fun and more, without expense and negative side effects,

I used to drink beer whenever I played golf. After getting saved, I found out I wasn't that bad of a golf player. Playing sober was more enjoyable, and I lost a lot less golf balls (yet another cost associated with drinking).

Benefits from stopping drinking and smoking alone include decreased chances of sickness like liver disease and cancer and saving money. And there are no drawbacks. The Bible tells us "The god of this world," (Satan), has blinded the eyes of those who don't believe (2 Corinthians 4:4). Once the blinders were removed from my eyes, I saw that the drawbacks keeping people from accepting Christ really aren't there.

POWER AND KNOWLEDGE/ "GOD JR."

In Ephesians 3:19, Paul prays the church will "be filled with all the fullness of God." I John 4:15 states, "Whosoever shall confess that Jesus is the Son of God, God dwelleth in him, and he in God."

What are the characteristics of God? He is loving, merciful, all knowing, and all powerful. What is the effect on us if we receive these characteristics? God is so powerful that, at the beginning of time, he made light shine out of darkness. When he is in us, all power is in us. God created man who invented science, mathematics, airplanes, nuclear bombs, etc. It's commonly said that people don't use even 10% of their brain. If God, who knows everything, is in you, you know everything. In 2 Corinthians 4:7, it says we have "this treasure in earthen vessels." What does this mean? Humans are limited. Our minds, bodies, and lives are limited. Yet the Holy Spirit allows this magnificent power and knowledge that is unlimited to enter our bodies, which are fragile by comparison.

We cannot hold it all at once. But we have access to whatever is needed. If I suddenly downloaded all the knowledge in the universe into my mind, who knows what would happen? I can't download the entire internet onto my laptop. If I could, I wouldn't know what to do with it. It would be unmanageable. But I can navigate the internet and access certain parts, as needed. The Holy Spirit is similar. It brings things to our mind/remembrance. It's also a teacher. Therefore, it can teach me something today, through whatever medium it wishes, turn around, and bring it to my remembrance tomorrow, or fifty years later.

Most people don't get the chance to have a personal relationship with the world's most powerful people, but we all can have a relationship with God. Knowledge of the Bible is power. To know it is to know God. In Hebrews 10:7, Christ said, "... Lo, I come (in the volume of the book it is written of me,) to do thy will, O God." The word of God is powerful. John 5:36 says it's quick (alive) and sharper than any two-edged sword. So, if I've studied the Bible and have the Holy Spirit, not only do I have access to powerful knowledge and ability to separate truth from lies, but I have a supernatural memory aid/recorder that plays the parts back I need at the appropriate times.

Applying the right scriptures will open spiritual eyes, change situations and remove things that need to be removed. In Isaiah 55:11, God says his word won't return empty or void. Therefore, all God's word will accomplish a divine purpose. Whatever God says is already done. It's a matter of time until it is revealed.

He sent his word out to protect, prosper, give rest, peace, and defeat my enemies. But for it to work effectively in my life toward my specific purpose, I must receive it and believe it. If my rich uncle in Cleveland dies and leaves me a million dollars, but I never read the will or make any effort to claim it, I won't receive anything. I must find out what I've been given and take action to cash in on what God has sat aside for me!

04

JUST SAY THE WORD

Our ears and eyes are gateways into our soul. The Holy Ghost is a gatekeeper. We all need to discern information properly to make good decisions for positive outcomes in our lives. The Holy Spirit is essential because the devil consistently uses people around us, including loved ones, media, and technology, to deliver lies to our doorstep. We're constantly subjected to huge amounts of wrong information, much of which could be fatal if acted upon. Because lies can sound good and are presented in a desirable way, some lies are impossible to identify as false if we haven't properly studied the Bible and have effective communication with our creator. Some of the biggest vehicles for harmful information over the past hundred years have been movies, music, and television. The devil uses these mediums to convey false messages and images, especially to young people. A single song can drive home a false message repeated over and over to hundreds of thousands of people.

Wrong messages are communicated so effectively because they are usually presented in a way that sounds good. And they can be hard to pick up on, because people often are not observant enough to realize they're false. Or if they do realize, they might dismiss it as not being a big deal. The song "Carry On Wayward Son," written in the 70s by the group Kansas, is one of the best sounding songs I've heard—and a total lie. "Wayward" has similar meaning to "contrary, obstinate," and "perverse." The song, in beautiful harmony, encourages a son to continue on a "wayward" path and says there will be "peace" when he's done with that. What a false guarantee! Who in their right mind would encourage a child they love to be contrary, obstinate, or perverse? Those don't lead to peace. It sounds great, but if the son in the song should die on the path the father is encouraging, he will never have peace. Literally, NEVER.

Aside from other negative impacts, a lot of messages and images serve to desensitize people. How many times have we heard someone say they don't listen to the lyrics of a catchy song, but they "just like the beat"? This is humanly impossible. The brain is a constant recorder keeping an ongoing history—consciously and unconsciously—of everything the person experienced since before they were even born. People are deceived when they don't acknowledge that words have power. And exposing oneself to those words, especially over and over, allows that power to work in their life, whether for good or bad.

The human mind is the greatest computer ever made. It automatically processes data and files it away. The data is inevitably called back up when a situation arises that the brain associates with the information on file. This can cause terrible, harmful decisions when the information the brain receives is false, and the brain doesn't know that.

A false statement frequently told to young girls and women is, "When you find the right guy for you, you'll just know." With the emotional and hormonal changes felt by young women, combined with the instability of inexperience, what could be farther from the truth? If they don't find something more stable and objective than their feelings to go by, they are likely to experience pain and make more mistakes than there needs to be.

John 8:44 says the devil is the "father of lies." Because his purpose is to rob and enslave people, he can't tell the truth. Because he's sneaky and cunning, misinformation designed by the devil isn't usually blatant, but often deceptive and hard to detect. Some misinformation is more obvious, but it's usually difficult because it might (1) sound good (i.e., rhyme or be set to catchy music), (2) appeal to emotion, (3) have been accepted for a long time, or (4) come from a trusted source. The dilemma is, with so many messages and images being sent and received, how do we separate the truth from lies?

If we rely on our own intelligence, we're in trouble because our hearts are (1) deceitful and (2) wicked (Jeremiah 17:9: "The heart is deceitful above all things, and desperately wicked; who can know it?")

Proverbs 14:12 says, "There is a way that seemeth [continues to seem] right unto a man but the end thereof are the ways of death." I cannot spell it out clearer. If we depend on ourselves, we're heading for serious trouble. Humans are changeable, emotional, and unstable. God, however, lets us know that "I change not" (Samuel 21:13). He is the same "yesterday, today and forever," (Isaiah 40:8, Hebrews 13:8). His word is absolute and eternal. We've gained technology, and people and cultures have drifted farther and closer to God at various times. Ecclesiastes 1:9 (NIV) says, "What has been will be again, what has been done will be done again; there is nothing new under the sun."

God's word and human nature are the same as they've been. As a result, if God ever said something, it's settled, even if it doesn't seem like it. Time doesn't apply to God. He exists outside of it and sees all historical and future events holistically at the same time. John 1:1 tells us that in the beginning, God and his word were inseparable. That means they're still inseparable today.

People often refer to themselves or others as someone who will "never change." A lot of popular songs over the years have claimed the singer or writer won't change. This is a red flag. The person is being dishonest, or more likely, deceived. With people, the only constant is change. They're constantly getting older, having experiences, and learning new information. Anyone who doesn't think they're constantly being molded or that they're totally formed and won't change is deceived.

They continue to be molded in different ways, even if they don't know it. We often hear that as people get older, they use less of a "filter" and are more outspoken. This proves that even the elderly are subject to change.

The Bible is the one true yardstick we have that is right and does not change. However, the devil has set up temptations and tricks to lure us off the path God has laid out for us before the beginning of time. These tricks and temptations include money, sex, drugs, alcohol, emotions, pride, and any one of the false messages the devil broadcasts daily. If we can identify wrong and destructive messages, we can make a conscious decision not to accept them. We must be watchful about what we allow to enter through our ears, eyes, and other senses. Many people who have found themselves in horrible situations may look back and wonder how they got there. Many times, the path to ruin began with looking or listening to something that opened the door to death, trouble, separation, and destruction.

Ephesians 4:27 says not to "give place to the devil." He's the ultimate example, for if you give him an inch, he takes a mile. When we become aware that a song, statement, situation, etc., conflicts with the Bible, it's in our best interest to reject it as early as possible. Some trouble is inevitable. But by being watchful, we can decrease and eliminate a lot of things we don't need to go through. In 1 Corinthians 10:13, it says no temptation has happened to anyone that isn't common to everyone, and with every temptation, God provides a way of escape. The problem is when people get so focused on the temptation instead of the Bible, they can't see the way to escape; and sometimes they just don't want to.

When problems happen, one of the first things many people ask is, "why me?" But rich, poor, Asian, Black, White, male, female—all encounter similar obstacles and distractions designed to move them outside the position where God wants them to be. God has created a way to escape from every negative situation (Joshua 23:14). No one can help us like God because he knows all historical backgrounds and future events. He also knows us better than we know ourselves, and, in the form of Jesus, he dealt with temptations while in the weakened human state but did not sin (Hebrews 2:18).

The answer to every problem we'll ever have is already figured out and even written so we can always know what to do. But instead of using this resource (Bible) which is available to everyone, we consult friends, family members, get advice from television, famous people, and many sources put in place to trick us, controlled by the enemy on a mission to destroy us. Or we try to figure things out on our own because we're deceived into thinking higher of our own intelligence than we should, and mislead ourselves into thinking we're smart enough to handle things. Because no problems are new, instead of trying to "reinvent the wheel," if one needs a solution, all they really need to figure out is what God, through the Bible, has already said about a given situation.

We are currently living in the most deceptive time in history. Following the September 11th tragedy, economic downturn, bird flu, swine flu and other epidemics, many people are scared. Isaiah 33:6 says knowledge and wisdom will be the stability of our times. If we don't have a relationship with God through the Bible, we'll be unstable in these deceptive and trying times.

No one knows exactly when Jesus is returning (Mark 13:32). Revelation 19 paints a vivid and awesome picture. When Jesus returns, the baby who slept in a manger and came to let people spit on him, hit him, pull his beard out, and ultimately kill him, while he didn't fight back—that will be over. He is coming back as an all-powerful judge. The entire world is going to court. Everyone who ever lived will be on time for that meeting. If someone knew they had a court date to go in front of a judge, if given a chance to meet and spend time with the judge beforehand, they'd do it. Yet people neglect the Bible. And every day, they neglect the opportunity to talk with and get closer to God.

05

SATAN—EMPLOYEE OF THE MILLENNIUM: HUMANS— ASLEEP ON THE JOB

Satan started out as a powerful and beautiful angel (Isaiah 14:12). He was the best musician in heaven. But like many people in high places, he fell. Hard. After he was thrown out of heaven, God didn't go after him or try to get him back. But when Adam sinned, God went looking for him (Genesis 3:9). God's love for man and the blessings he's provided for them are so great and such a mystery that the angels desire to look into it (1 Peter 1:12). Romans 8:13 says as many as are led by God's spirit are the sons of God; not some day in the future, but now. Human beings, whose bodies are fragile and minds often filled with fear and confusion, have received the opportunity to be adopted into God's family (Romans 8:15). This is much better than being adopted by a rich family who might have a couple of mansions and vacation homes. God owns the entire universe! This is an opportunity not always available before Jesus's death. Hebrews 2:3 asks, "How shall we escape if we neglect so great salvation?"

Picture the devil in an office working non-stop. He's under a deadline. His mission statement is up on the wall, "Kill, steal and destroy" (John 10:10). The devil's job is to get people to neglect salvation. It's a high stakes job. He works on commission (souls) and is highly motivated and skilled at his job. Satan does it by trying to get people to neglect, not believe and go against God's word. He does his homework and knows every person way better than they know themselves. He influences people to be pre-occupied and focus on things that don't matter in the big picture. And he tells them that all the suffering he's caused, which man has allowed, is God's fault. Satan is lost forever. No one can ever save him. He is headed for hell and wants to take people with him because he hates God and we're made in the image of God (Genesis 1:26–27). If one doesn't; (1) realize the devil is busy and (2) is too tricky for humans, they've already been deceived.

I can use my own logic with information received through my five senses to arrive at what seems like good moral decisions. And that might seem to work for a while, but it leads to death (separation from God). It's a natural tendency to rely on our limited thinking instead of the Bible. Once we get into that pattern, we can't get out of it by ourselves. We must be born again (John 3:3). When that happens, the old things pass away (2 Corinthians 5:17). It takes God to turn us around. And it's important to remember there's no guarantee he will continue to pursue any person past any point. He gave people free will and made the Bible available to everyone. He also provided pastors and teachers (that love and care for us) after his own heart, Each person has made the personal decision to accept or reject all of that. Hebrews 2: 3-4 NLT says, "3 So what makes us think we can escape if we ignore this great salvation that was first announced by the Lord Jesus himself and then delivered to us by those who heard him speak? 4 And God confirmed the message by giving signs and wonders and various miracles and gifts of the Holy Spirit whenever he chose." God knows every person's heart and already knows how that person will respond to his repeated knocks at their heart-door. Free will is a beautiful and terrifying thing.

I had to come to the knowledge and understanding that my opinion doesn't mean anything. Despite extensive education, I'm not that smart. I know just enough to be dangerous. That danger can extend to those around me, including my children, other family members, and anybody who follows me. There are always people watching and following us, whether or not we're aware of it. Luckily for us, a good God who didn't leave us defenseless made us. He gave us weapons, gifts, and his word to deal with every situation correctly and be a positive influence on all those we come in contact with.

Jesus was the ultimate role model. Though he was the eternal God and creator of the universe, entering the weak, fleshly body enabled him to be tempted in the same ways as every other human (Hebrews 4:15). The Bible tells us Jesus was tempted by the devil himself who came and tried to get him to do foolish things (such as bow down to the devil and jump off a cliff) at a time when Jesus was weak from hunger (Matthew 4:6, Luke 4:9). How did Jesus respond? He didn't shoot him with a fireball, perform miracles, or challenge him to a fight. He quoted appropriate Bible scriptures and after a few attempts; the devil left.

If we watch the local news, we see and hear about tragedy after tragedy engineered by the devil. We could avoid many if we only recognized what was going on and spoke/applied appropriate Bible passages in faith. The Bible says the word of God is alive and that it's a weapon, sharper than a sword Hebrew 4:12. The power of the word of God made the whole earth and, when applied in faith, has mighty power to change situations. It's the ultimate weapon. Jesus illustrated how to use that weapon, which resulted in eternal life, victory, and the devil running away.

I recently saw a news report about a man shot to death by police after he led them on a chase on the freeway. I recall he was wanted for rape, among other things. The reckless car chase placed many innocent people in danger. I thought maybe it was a good thing that they killed the man because of the harm and danger he was causing to the community. But Ephesians 6:12 and 2 Corinthians 10:3–6 say we don't fight against flesh (people), but against unseen spirits and powers. The person who committed the crimes had little to do with what was going on except that he was making himself available to be used by evil, destructive spirits. It's obvious he didn't plan very well. The human brain is smart enough to know the likely results of things like violent crimes and police chases. He was very irrational, some would say, insane. Insanity is real, but it doesn't explain the driving force that motivates a lot of evil acts. The word of God will override those motivating forces.

What influences people to act against their own best interest, all the way to committing suicide? It's not so much them, but the fact something else came in and took over their thinking. Common sense and logic aren't in control. No one in their "right mind" would do a lot of the harmful things people do. Murder-suicide, drug abuse, and all disobedience/sin, results from letting the devil come in. When someone gives him an inch, he tries to take over. In simple terms, at the root of all sin, illogical and immoral actions, Satan led the person to believe a lie which didn't begin at the moment or day they committed the act. For example, a seventy-five-year-old dying of emphysema or lung cancer may have started off at three years old watching a television role model or father figure who smoked and decided it was something they wanted to do. At the heart of every sin is the fact that at some point, the person entertained a lie. Unfortunately, every lie leads to a bigger one. With each one, the individual ignores the voice of God, often labeled as "conscience." The voice gradually gets harder to hear, and the person sinks lower and lower. The result, if the person doesn't turn around, is death.

People who commit crimes and heinous acts are generally no worse or better than anyone else. They act according to a spirit that entered, possibly through a parent, song, movie, friend, etc. That spirit called friends to join them, and they took over. When a human being is physically destroyed, controlling evil spirits don't die with the person.

Nor do they just retire. Within minutes, they're looking for an entrance into the life of the next person they can influence.

From the beginning, God gave man authority over the earth, water, and air (Genesis 1:26), but we're not doing a good job policing it. Evil influences come and go almost freely, and the only thing that can effectively fight or keep them out is prayer and people who know God's word. In the beginning, the earth was nothing until God said, "Let there be light," and the other things and systems he so perfectly spoke into existence. That demonstrates the awesome creative power of God's word. It's more important than food because it created the world and sustains all of the earth's systems. It's the glue keeping earth and the stars in place, holding all of our bodies together. Once I came to this realization, I developed new respect and motivation to learn the Bible. After studying it, I learned it has the answer to every problem I'll ever face.

I used to fear I'd die before my children were grown. I wanted to write an instruction booklet to leave them about things I'd learned to look out for, avoid, how to handle situations, etc. Then I realized it was already done, not just for them, but for everyone. God's word, the Bible, never changes or loses its power or effectiveness.

John 1:1 says that in the beginning, the word was with God, and the word actually *was* God. This is a hard—if not impossible—concept to understand without help from the Holy Spirit; the concept that we cannot separate God and his word. As a result, the one impossible thing for God to do is lie. This is terrific news because the Bible is packed with awesome promises. But we can't take advantage of them unless we know what they are. Once we find out and believe, we become aware we can never die, we can recover from any disease, and we don't have to worry about jobs, homes, children, what we'll wear, eat, etc. We will realize the authority and responsibility we have to police foul and evil spirits that cause murder, suicide, terrorism, child rape, the list goes on and on.

I estimate ninety-some percent of people live beneath their privilege because they don't know who they are and what is supernaturally available to them. Most Americans don't like or fully understand the concept of a king, because we pride ourselves on independence, the idea of freedom, and a democratic system where we vote for a president. But no matter how anyone feels about it, God is the king of *everything*. A king's power is absolute. They answer to no one. Nobody can veto what they want to do. They can't be voted down. They are respected and feared for their power and position. In ancient times, you couldn't even go near a king unless he sent for you. If you approached him on your own, he had to hand you his staff or his knights/security killed you. End of story.

Most people today don't realize the privilege of living after Jesus. Hebrews 4:16 says we can now not only approach God's throne (through prayer), we can do it "boldly." If most people could spend time with a president, they'd be excited and couldn't wait. They'd get a haircut, carefully plan their outfit and what they were going to say. They'd tell their family and friends and would have a lot of excitement the night before. But most people waste the opportunity to approach the one who made the president. Why? Because they (1) don't know or believe God's word and (2) prefer to follow what they can physically see and understand instead of what God said. In John 20:29, Jesus, after he rose from the dead, told Thomas, "Because you have seen me you have believed. Blessed are those who have not seen, and have believed." Everybody who ever lived will see Jesus and bow to him (Romans 14:11). But by the time they actually see him, they won't have a *choice* to believe. But those who realize beforehand that, even though they can't see him, there's an obvious architect of the water, sky, trees, oxygen, carbon dioxide, etc., and seek a relationship with him—those are blessed. In 2 Corinthians 4:18, it says the things we see are temporary, but the things unseen last forever. So, if one is trusting in a house, car, money, or another human being, it's only a matter of time until they're going to be let down.

When the devil tempted Jesus himself, he tried to get him to doubt his identity (Matthew 4:11). Ignorance or doubt about identity is one of the major problems today. Satan fights hard to suppress it because once we know and understand it, we are an enormous threat to him and his mission to rob, kill, and destroy. One of the first teaching series my wife and I sat through after we received the Holy Spirit was about adoption; that when you accept Christ, you enter a royal family. This adoption has many rights and responsibilities—all clearly spelled out—and the benefits far outweigh the obligations. The word of God is the most powerful thing on earth. It made the earth. When we believe it and repeat it (pray) back to God, he responds (Mark 11:22–25).

06

ALL AUTHORITY COMES FROM GOD

Jesus then came out, wearing the crown of thorns and the purple robe. Pilate said to them, "Behold, the Man!" So when the chief priests and the officers saw Him, they cried out saying, "Crucify, crucify!" Pilate said to them, "Take Him yourselves and crucify Him, for I find no guilt in Him." The Jews answered him, "We have a law, and by that law He ought to die because He made Himself out to be the Son of God." Therefore when Pilate heard this statement, he was even more afraid; and he entered into the Praetorium again and said to Jesus, "Where are You from?" But Jesus gave him no answer. Then saith Pilate unto him, Speakest thou not unto me? knowest thou not that I have power to crucify thee, and have power to release thee? Jesus answered him, "You have no authority over me at all, except what was given to you from above. That's why the one who handed me over to you is guilty of a greater sin" (John 19:5–11, NIV).

The beginning of the Iraq war in 2003 emotionally affected me. I was downright distraught. I couldn't believe *my* country was going to invade another country and kill people based on reasoning that didn't make sense. I was in disbelief and frustrated. Then I talked to my mother about it and will always be thankful for the knowledge she brought to my attention. I will never forget the peace it gave me, and it has been a great help in various areas of my life.

She pointed out that unjustified war was not new, and more importantly, the President and those in charge could do *nothing* more than the Lord allowed them to. It put my mind at ease and put things in perspective. After being saved, I learned more about it and the understanding of authority changed my life. For example, I realized that at work, many things are above my pay range, and it is up to others to decide and figure out.

As a Christian, I have a duty to pray for him, but the president's actions aren't my responsibility. He's not unchecked. He's very much in check. Things that seem very out of control really aren't. Even when people act outside God's will, he's able to plan around it and make it ultimately work out for good. And I should sleep well after praying and knowing the situation is in God's hands. The president's actions are not my responsibility to worry about, and God has actually commanded me not to stress about it (Proverbs 21:1 and Philippians 4:6).

In my younger days, I wasn't a strict rule follower. I often instituted my own judgment, evaluated rules through my own lens of critical thinking, not knowing or recognizing God was behind them, or at the very least, permitted them. I liked rules that seemed necessary and sensible. Others that seemed like nonsense or too much hassle I'd follow part of the time, or routinely complain (complaining is forbidden Philippians 2:14).

At times in my professional career, I reported to people who I didn't think knew as much as I did. Some seemed unintelligent. My reaction and attitude toward instruction that didn't make sense to me was poor. My inappropriate outlook toward rules and authority had a negative effect on my performance and quality of work. I wasn't operating according to Colossians 3:23, which says, "Whatsoever ye do, do [it] heartily, as to the Lord, and not unto men."

Romans 12:3 says every man is "not to think [of himself] more highly than he ought to think." In this context, thinking of yourself more highly than the authority God put over us is to think of ourselves higher than we ought to. It was God who saw fit to put the authority in place. It didn't just happen. All authority works toward a divine purpose. It's out of order to think more highly of oneself than one who has been placed over you because of the simple fact they were placed over you. It's a simple matter of position. IQ, knowledge, etc., have nothing to do with it. If someone is over you, God knows about it. He knows all things and allowed them to be there. He knows everyone who will ever be over you your whole life and allowed it for a reason.

So, except for in extreme cases (i.e., where it might break the law, endanger someone, etc.,), you have a choice and responsibility to submit to the highest authority. If there's a conflict, it's the responsibility of the subordinate to change as directed. Everyone is a subordinate to someone. After you've done what you're supposed to do, if there's still a problem or injustice, God will deal with it appropriately (just remember his ways are higher than our ways). If someone addresses things their own way, any blame will rest on them—God's hands are somewhat tied from being able to step in because they sought their own solution. They've rejected God's plan in favor of what they thought.

Whether one rejects or submits to authority isn't hidden to those around them. We can see it in their attitude and how they carry out tasks. After I learned God was the actual source of all authority, I stopped working to impress people and managers, so much as God himself. "When a man's ways please the Lord, he maketh even his enemies to be at peace with him" (Proverbs 16:7). Put another way, when people do what God said and handle things his way, it makes everyone be at peace with them, even their enemies!

Bosses can be moody and change from day to day. They sometimes make promises they later forget. If I focused on that, I'd develop a negative attitude. But when I focus on God, who is ultimately in control and doesn't change, I can be happy and do consistent good work. Once

I learned this, I became immune to office politics, budget cuts, and the attitudes of people around me. No matter what goes on around me, I can stay the same and do consistently good work with a positive attitude, because I really am working for God. He's ultimately the source of the paycheck and the one who allowed me to get hired in the first place. If somebody lies to me or tries to take credit for my work, God sees it. Even if I'm treated badly, I can be respectful because I know the Lord won't let it go on forever. He even works bad things out for good (Romans 8:28). And, if I continue to do what I'm supposed to with the right attitude, God can and will work on my behalf.

Wise people recognize God is orderly and hierarchical. There's a huge, unseen organizational chart. Everybody from janitors to the president ultimately report to God and are accountable to him. If my manager doesn't treat me right, I don't have to worry—they will ultimately answer to God.

If someone does something to me, it's not my responsibility to get them back. I don't have the authority or the right ("vengeance is mine; I will repay saith the Lord," Romans 12:19). If someone wrongs me, I should first ask myself if there's something I should've done differently. Then it's helpful to consider, "Am I better off letting God handle what he has said was his? Or ignore him and try my own way? Am I blinded by anger and pride enough to think I can do God's job better than he can?" This is a classic example of how people get deceived by pride and emotion, often from lack of knowledge of or not being reminded of God's word. Nothing good can come from disobeying God (except repentance). People react with revenge when somebody wrongs them by trying to get the person back, ultimately putting themself in the dangerous and harmful position of being disobedient.

Poor attitude and lack of understanding can cause people to play right into the devil's plans. I believe there are some poor managers who count on employees not following directions—then they can come down on them if and whenever they choose to do so. They can let them go a long time and possibly never bring the subject up, or choose to do so at a time convenient for them. This behavior can give enemies the power to bring you down at any point. I have spent time and energy trying to work around bad policies and instructions. This brought stress and frustration I shouldn't have had because it wasn't my responsibility. I wasn't staying in a position to say unequivocally that "I did what I was told." I didn't realize that by not following instructions and coming up with my own ways to do things, I was taking on management responsibilities without the pay. As a result, if it didn't work, it would be my fault. I was putting pressure on myself that belonged to someone else. This was stressful, much to the devil's enjoyment, I'm sure.

Shortly after I received the Holy Spirit and gave my life to God, a manager at work who didn't seem to like me instructed me loudly one morning to sign in and out of work at the *exact* time I came in and out. I believe she thought I wouldn't listen. The work rules said, in addition to a grace period for arriving late, employees could arrive up to ten minutes early. Based on prior practice, I previously signed in at 8:00 a.m. regardless of whether I was within ten minutes early or late. The directive to sign in at the *exact* time applied to arriving early and working late. As a result, if I arrived ten minutes early each day, by the end of the week, I could have almost an hour extra, requiring me to leave early on Friday or need to be paid overtime. Who knew? What she meant to single me out wound up being a benefit. Prior to being saved, I might have resisted and focused on why I was being singled out. But by being obedient, I walked out ahead of my co-workers with a clear conscience.

God is a God of order. He placed those —or allowed those leaders to be placed—over me for a reason. As long as I honor him (includes respecting decisions I don't understand), he must help me, protect me, and deal with my problems. If I am mistreated, he will handle it; maybe not at the exact time or way I want, but in his perfect way and time.

Daniel 2:21 says God "removeth kings, and setteth up kings" (by today's standards this can mean presidents, CEOs, etc.).

Romans 13:1–2 says all authority comes from God; "Let every soul be subject unto the higher powers. For there is no power but of God; the powers that be are ordained of God. Whosoever therefore resisteth the power, resisteth the ordinance of God." When I disregard God and do things my own flawed way, I set myself up as lord over my life. This disables God from helping because he's not going to support and encourage my flawed thinking and behavior—I'd probably become a tyrant. When we go outside of the rules God sat up for us, there are consequences. "Be not deceived; God is not mocked: for whatsoever a man soweth, that shall he also reap" Galatians 6:7.

Since coming into this knowledge, my quality of work and life improved a lot. My attitude and job performance are greatly improved. I am less stressed because, by ignoring instructions, I was taking on extra responsibilities. I greatly enjoy going to work now. My change is evidence that God's way is better. "For as the heavens are higher than the earth, so are my ways higher than your ways, and my thoughts than your thoughts" Isaiah 55:9. Doing things God's way brings positive results, which boosts faith, which brings more peace and positive results, setting up positive cycles in people's lives.

07

EVERYTHING'S GOING MY WAY—ALL THINGS WORK TOGETHER FOR THE GOOD OF THOSE WHO LOVE THE LORD

As previously mentioned, I once tried to compete with sneaky people at work. I wasn't very good at it, but it seemed like the thing to do. Now I rest and know all they're doing is digging themselves a hole only God can get them out of. All situations work out in my favor when I trust God, regardless of how the situation looks. "And we know that all things work together for good to them that love God" (Romans 8:28). "All" covers everything, even plans to destroy us or cause trouble. This is a reassuring concept, though not easy for the human mind to accept, because it's our nature to want to understand and make sense of everything. The creation of our bodies and the world we're living in are proof that many important things are beyond our ability to understand. Even evil plans against me will help me out. So, I might as well relax. This can be difficult because our nature is to fight back, seek revenge, protect ourselves, and things of that nature. Second Corinthians 5:7 says we walk by faith, not by sight. This means I believe in the Bible despite what my brain, emotions, or people around me say.

There's a lot of widely accepted advice that directly conflicts with the Bible. How many times have well-meaning friends or parents told a young person to "follow their heart"? Yet, as mentioned before, the Bible points out, "The human heart is the most deceitful of all things, and desperately wicked. Who really knows how bad it is?" (Jeremiah 17:9, NLT). Faith increases by hearing (when we read, we hear in our mind) what the Bible says. Once we know the word, we can walk in faith. No matter how bad circumstances appear, if we stay in faith, they work out in our favor—100% of the time. It seems too good to be true. If we don't see results almost immediately, though, we tend to doubt. When we do see clear results, our minds want to rationalize it as coincidence. This is the battle of the mind: flesh vs. spirit (limited finite part of ourselves vs. spirit; tangible vs. unseen).

When I was young, I viewed the Bible as restrictive. But it's basically just God's wisdom in written form. Proverbs 23:23 says "Buy the truth, and sell it not; Also wisdom, and instruction, and understanding." Trying to go through life without wisdom is like putting together complicated furniture without reading the directions—you're sure to make mistakes and leave important things out that will lead to problems later. We make many mistakes because we don't know what we don't know. Isaiah 33:6 says, "Wisdom and knowledge shall be the stability of thy times." When I was passed over for promotion at work, I was stable, knowing that I worked for God more than people, that he loves me and is responsible for me.

I'm not a huge fan of everything Woody Hayes, former Ohio State football coach from 70s, did. But I believe he was right when he said, if something's easy, it's not worth a darn (didn't actually say "darn"). Serving God isn't easy. It requires us to go against what we want when the Bible says we should. This requires us to be tested. Galatians 6:9 states we shall reap in due season if we don't faint (stop). Romans 12:2

says not to be conformed to this world, but transformed; in other words, don't let the things around us mold and influence us to go against God. Being saved occurs the instant we receive Christ as the head of our life (he then becomes responsible for us), but the transformation of our minds—correcting the improper ways we've learned to think—takes a lifetime. It's not easy for humans to change, even when it's obviously for the better. Example: Cigarettes say on the package they will kill you, but people still start all the time and find it difficult to quit. Drug addicts can be seen living unhappily in filth, yet new people experiment with drugs every day.

Even the trials we go through are *all* for our good after we accept Jesus. It's like gold and silver refining. The impurities separate and burn away in hot temperatures, leaving behind the best and most valuable part. After we are saved, there are attributes God needs to change and bring out of us. Through trials, God brings us to a higher place where he can use us and bless us more. To go back to the smoking example— it's God's will for us to have perfect health. Would it make sense for him to heal, intervene, and bless us with total good health while we are smoking six packs of cigarettes per day? Maybe. But because he's a parent (the ultimate father), we often must do something for him to give us things we want and things he wants us to have in order for it not to be harmful. If we don't know or are unwilling to do what's in our own interest, like a good parent, he sometimes has to let us be uncomfortable or wait for us to mature before giving us things he really wants us to have. Once entrusted to us, he wants us to be able to maintain it.

HELP AND COMFORT

One of the toughest tests for my wife Angel and I began a few months after I was saved, about one year into our marriage, when I experienced the death of three close family members in five months. My aunt Joyce, who was like a sister growing up, was diagnosed with cancer around Christmas and died in January. I will never forget my mother's strength to stand and sing so strongly and beautifully at her funeral. It took strength I didn't know she had, supplied no doubt, by the Holy Spirit. I was with Aunt Joyce when she died, almost a year to the day after my wedding. It was the hardest thing I had to deal with since my grandmother died when I was seven. But Joyce hadn't been feeling well for several months, so it wasn't completely unexpected. But the loss a couple of weeks later, on February 12, 2008, caught us totally by surprise.

Even as Joyce's life wound down, she was excited about Angel being pregnant with our daughter Grace. I had four boys from a previous marriage, who Joyce dearly loved, but her eyes lit up at the thought of having a little girl around! One Monday, Angel had gone to the hospital for a check-up. I was in a long meeting at work. About 10:30 a.m. my cell phone rang several times in a row. When I called Angel back, she was hysterical. She told me to get to the hospital as soon as I could. They couldn't find Grace's heartbeat. I mumbled to my manager and hustled out of the meeting in a fog. Luckily, I only had to walk two blocks to get to the one place in the city where taxis were readily available. Twenty-five minutes later, I got to the hospital. Angel was crying. Her following eight hours of labor before she gave birth to a stunning, perfectly formed, twenty-one-inch long baby girl, stillborn from an umbilical cord accident, was the most courageous thing I'd ever seen.

I'd always considered myself a loner who didn't need people (a false idea I later learned wasn't biblical). But I'll never forget the peace and comfort from the presence of so many church members and friends present at the graveside service for my perfect daughter I got to meet for only a few hours. She was flawlessly formed and forever silent in this world. Through the power of the Holy Spirit, I stood up and read Psalm 34:1, "I will bless the Lord at all times: his praise shall continually be in my mouth."

To end the string of departures, my grandfather, "Gramps" died Memorial Day weekend three months later at 93 years old. His health had declined over several years and particularly during the final few months. He was an old-fashioned person who valued hard work and independence. Widely regarded as an honest and "good" person, he did things his own way until finally relenting in November 2007, when I was privileged to baptize him in Jesus's name under guidance of Pastor Junior Walker at Apostolic Pentecostal Tabernacle in Chesterhill, Ohio. Gramps's life remains a testament to God's mercy, love and long suffering. People had been praying for his salvation for thirty or forty years, maybe longer, and the Lord allowed him to live to be baptized just six months before he died. It wasn't easy helping him in and out of the baptismal pool—his strength and mobility had dropped considerably, and he still weighed well over two hundred pounds.

My aunt Joyce was a "daddy's girl" who had a learning disability that kept her from living and functioning independently, away from home. She had a job once decades ago, but one day she came home crying for some reason that might have been soon forgotten, but Gramps told her she didn't need to go back. So, she stayed at home and especially after my grandmother passed away, he became the biggest part of her world.

A few days before Joyce went into the hospital not to return home, Gramps fell while my mom was at work and Joyce called 911. Gramps left in an ambulance, never to return to the home he loved and lived in for so for many years. He was a proud man who poured concrete for a living and did hard labor into his 80s. I'd always envisioned he'd never leave the house he'd built with his own hands. I'd always figured he might die working.

It's an understatement to say Gramps wasn't thrilled to be in a nursing home. But looking back, with the help of the Holy Spirit, I see it was likely necessary to get him out of his comfort zone to depend totally on God. Except while in the army during World War II, it was probably one of the only times in his adult life he wasn't in total control of his surroundings. That undoubtedly humbled him to help accept Christ in a way he otherwise might not have.

I'm forever thankful God saved me prior to losing so many family members. It helped me get through it, but more importantly, the Holy Spirit enabled me to comfort, pray for, and truly help them in meaningful ways. Looking back, prior to receiving the Holy Spirit, I could provide some comfort by being there and doing small things like getting someone a cup of water or some ice chips. But the Holy Spirit reveals to us what people *really* need and helps us pray effectively to meet those needs and get results. Without it, I couldn't do much but be present and perhaps act tough, as though I could physically beat cancer, a weak heart, or old age.

The last time I talked to Gramps, the words I said were so perfect, I never could've come up with them on my own without help from the Holy Spirit. He seemed depressed about his lack of strength; I don't think he ever foresaw a day when he couldn't work, let alone walk. The Holy Spirit spoke through me to tell him everyone has to rest sometimes. No one works forever. Even God rested.

Gramps was very attentive that day and the last thing I said to him was that I had to go get ready for work tomorrow, but the Lord said he would *never* leave him or forsake him. There is a paved trail around the nursing home, and the Holy Spirit led me to march around it while praying in tongues. Romans 8:26-27 NLT says, "And the Holy Spirit helps us in our weakness. For example, we don't know what God wants us to pray for. But the Holy Spirit prays for us with groanings that cannot be expressed in words. And the Father who knows all hearts knows what the Spirit is saying, for the Spirit pleads for us believers in harmony with God's own will." I believe my grandfather was saved and will live in heaven for eternity. I get overwhelmed when I think about God's patience to lead Gramps to accept eternal life at such an old age and keep him around. That last day I read to him about the promised land flowing with milk and honey, and how the ones who believed God would deliver them were the ones who entered.

I am grateful and thank God I was able to comfort Joyce in her final days. She had a huge bottle of olive oil that the pastor had blessed. I'd sometimes get to her hospice room and see she was in pain or distress. I'd anoint her with the oil, pray, and see instant relief come over her. In her last hour, God showed me a Bible verse I don't recall ever having seen before or since. It was basically a guide for summoning angels. It was right on time! I believe she had a grand escort because I prayed God's word to him and believed he'd do what he said. I was hurting, and the Bible lets us know God feels our pain through Jesus. "For we have not a high priest which cannot be touched with the feeling of our infirmities…" Hebrews 4:15. I comforted Joyce beyond measure and helped influence my grandfather to come to Christ and accept eternal life during the last six months of his ninety-three years. I could not have done these things effectively if not for the power and leading of the Holy Spirit.

HEALING

Four months after Gramps's death, my mother became sick in September 2008. She went from doctor to doctor, and they ultimately believed she had cancer in her uterus, and likely also in one of her lungs. Exactly one year later, she went through many of the same appointments Joyce had. I prayed like I never prayed before. Throughout the process, God gave me signs that everything would be OK. The same day the doctors made the probable cancer diagnosis, she received a holiday card from some Christian relatives containing a scripture. I should but don't remember the exact scripture. I know it said God will restore health. A couple of days before Christmas, I took her to the hospital for a similar procedure

Joyce had the year before. During a six-hour surgery, doctors found no cancer anywhere but found another minor problem (which they were able to correct).

Besides healing/avoiding cancer and getting Mom's health back, I'll never forget what God did in the preparatory room before her surgery. The doctor scheduled it to be an all-day procedure. I believed God would heal her, but I had to prepare myself to accept God's will. It was a serious day for me. The prior year, Mom took Aunt Joyce for the same procedure, and she never made it back home. So, I took Mom on the same trip (though to a different hospital).

Mom had to go into a room where she got various IVs and they checked her levels of fluids, sugar, etc. After they placed her in the room, we were able to spend some time with her talking and praying, leading up to the surgery, which would take about six hours. About twenty minutes after we joined her in the room, nurses pulled a curtain closed, dividing the room, and put another patient on the other side to prepare for their procedure (seemingly minor). It sounded like the woman's entire extended family was there and they were the loudest and most vulgar group you could hope to meet.

Their profanity and behavior weren't what you'd expect from people in a hospital. Yet there they were, fifteen feet from us, separated by only a curtain. No subject matter was off limits (they worked details in their conversation about someone having oral sex, etc.). At first, I had a positive attitude. I'd been praying the entire morning and continued to pray. Early on, I even felt somewhat sorry for the family. But after the "F bombs" and vulgar references continued, I felt anger creeping up. Enough was enough! It was a familiar feeling I'd felt often before I accepted Christ. I heard another loud and nasty comment through the curtain, and I opened my mouth to confront them. At the exact same time I opened my mouth to speak, mom, sensing my frustration, spoke and asked me not to say anything. She shook her head and whispered, "Just pray."

Looking back, I realize my chances of reasoning with that family were pretty much non-existent. Trying to engage with them could have resulted in a major blow up—in a hospital of all places! I was very sensitive to the situation, and they clearly didn't care. Could you imagine my poor mother if she had to be stressed out by a big argument on her way into surgery? The devil would've been the only winner. Things could have escalated badly very quickly. Thank God he spoke through Mom when he did. Instead of engaging with them, I prayed for peace against the disruption.

All that day, we'd hoped Mom's pastor, and his wife would make it from their home two hours away before she went to the operating room. Less than five minutes after I started praying regarding the nightmare family, Pastor Walker and his wife arrived. They didn't waste time and immediately started praying for her. The atmosphere immediately changed. At some point, I realized it was totally silent on the other side of the curtain. With the power and anointing the Walkers released in the room, I believe the foul spirits found it hard to operate. I never heard another peep. At one point, I walked to the windowsill to grab my jacket and saw around the edge of the curtain. The ringleader of the cursing and crude comments had crawled up on the windowsill and was fast asleep, the exact result I'd hoped for! But because I waited and took the problem to God and didn't try to handle it on my own, I didn't have to do anything wrong—I didn't even have to speak! I received the desired result while keeping the peace.

I realize now as I write this what the devil was doing. He knew exactly where Pastor Walker and his wife were on the road, and he wanted to cause a negative atmosphere before they got there. I wouldn't have been able to join with them properly in faithful agreement while arguing and fighting at the same time. The devil was trying to create strife and confusion to get me out of position to pray and effectively be used by God. These people were under demonic control/attack and had no clue. If he can make strife and confusion before a good thing happens, the devil might be able to hinder a move of God. It's not that he has power to hinder God himself, but people can allow themselves to be moved out of position to be used for God's power to flow through them.

08

THE DANGER OF STRIFE— ARGUE WITH NO ONE

Hebrews 12:14 says to "follow peace with all men." The set-up at the hospital was just that. The devil uses his knowledge to set up unsuspecting people. It wasn't unknown to him that the group and me together in a small space under the circumstances was a terrible combination. It's important to remember the devil can't touch people. But he creates situations, gives people ideas, then sits back and watches the outcome. Believe it or not, he knows exactly how to "push your buttons." Fortunately, it didn't work at the hospital. I followed peace, and I stayed in the word. But what if I hadn't?

The things that could go wrong in a major surgery are many. Aside from the fact she needed supernatural protection and healing, doctors also needed divine help and guidance. Irreversible damage could happen if they didn't administer the anesthesia right. We needed God to oversee the people, process, and equipment. God doesn't operate in confusion and strife. "Let nothing be done through strife" (Philippians 2:3). Where the Lord can't work because of people not being obedient and submitting to him, the devil can be productive. His mission is to rob, steal, and kill.

Before accepting Christ, I didn't realize that throughout the years, every time I'd lose my temper and enter arguments and strife, I was shutting the door to God's ability to work my situation out in my favor his way. I was giving the devil room to mess up my life, cause problems, hurt family members and others. Because I avoided strife the day mom was in the hospital, the Lord handled things his way. If the devil can get his foot in the door, watch out! It's hard to get him out. When he gets an inch, he'll wreak havoc on situations, and people won't even realize what's happening or where it's coming from. Many times, he gains access through strife because, where confusion and turmoil are, he basically has authority to operate. Where peace is, God is. That's why the Bible says to "follow peace." Hebrews 12:14: "Follow peace with all men, and holiness, without which no man shall see the Lord."

The Bible warns against arguing with fools. "Do not answer a fool according to his folly, or you yourself will be just like him" (Proverbs 26:4, NIV). For me to have engaged the family at the hospital would've been an exercise in futility. They wouldn't have minded a big argument—they were already loud and arguing with each other anyway. They clearly weren't sensible. So what could I hope to gain by engaging them in a conversation, especially when I was already angry? The chances they'd have stopped what they were doing because I asked were very slim. Christianity points to Christ as the role model. Jesus didn't travel around engaging in arguments.

09

BE ANXIOUS ABOUT NOTHING

Philippians 4:6 (NLT) says, "Don't worry about anything; instead, pray about everything. Tell God what you need, and thank him for all he has done."

Since turning my life over to God, I've prayed a lot. It only makes sense if you have access to unlimited knowledge that you use it frequently, while giving praise and thanks to the one who provided it.

Proverbs 3:6 (KJV) says, "In all thy ways acknowledge him, and he shall direct thy paths." It's of utmost importance to take God at his word. It's easy to fall into human tendencies to substitute what we think and let our minds be deceived into accepting ideas that are different from God's word. If I'm obedient to his word and acknowledge him in everything, that includes situations that would otherwise cause worry and concern.

The Bible constantly reminds us that faith is the key to operating in God's kingdom. James 1:7 says for anyone who wavers in faith, not to expect to receive anything from God.

So that being said, after I've prayed to God about any issue, continuing to worry represents lack of belief that God will do what he said he'd do, such as work every situation out in my favor—"And we know that all things work together for good to them that love God, to them who are the called according to his purpose" (Romans 8:28).

Serving God should be an active exercise with faith. He's given us power and authority as well as responsibility to do certain things. Faith without works is dead (James 2:17). This means a true believer will do certain things for no other reason than because God's word said so. When a believer of the Bible acts, positive results follow. They have to; blessings have been ordained to follow acts of obedience the same way God commanded rivers to go into oceans.

Psalms 23:2 states he *maketh* me to lie down in green pastures. Though lying down in green pastures seems like a pleasant and comforting activity, humans tend to have rebellion against being made to do *anything*. God's rules aren't negotiable. He's not a respecter of people—his word applies to presidents, homeless people, and CEOs of companies.

God doesn't give two cents about anyone's opinion. Think about it. God made the earth and put people in charge, reporting to him. Science reveals we haven't even figured out how to use the full capacity of our own brains God gave us. As a result, it would make absolutely no sense for him to ask for advice or wonder what I think about a situation. My opinion doesn't matter and he already knows what I'd say anyway. If I have any wisdom, I understand how little I know. I must focus on my job and the only way I even know what my true job is, is by looking to God. Isaiah 45:9 NLT says, "What sorrow awaits those who argue with their Creator. Does a clay pot argue with its maker? Does the clay dispute with the one who shapes it, saying, 'Stop, you're doing it wrong!' Does the pot exclaim, 'How clumsy can you be?'"

When I told my young daughter the Bible says the wealth of wicked people is laid up for the just people (Proverbs 13:22), she instinctively questioned how that could be and how it operated. The answer is the same for her as it is for everyone—that we don't need to worry about *how* God's word will be fulfilled. His ways, after all, are higher than our ways and he can do exceedingly more than anything we can ask for or even think of (Isaiah 55:8).

His ways being "higher" means he sees more. We must come to the place of being like a little kid. If the parents of a three- or four-year-old promises them a new bike, the child usually doesn't ask, "Now wait a minute, how are you going to accomplish this? How will you pay for it? How will you get it here?" Most kids are just happy and expect the bike. And a good parent delivers the bike out of faithfulness, love and obligation to the child.

According to the website everydayhealth.com, manic-depressive people experience periods of very low depression followed by periods of frenzied, uncontrolled activity. This isn't the will of God in our lives. As mentioned before, Psalms 23 says his will forces us to lie down in a beautiful and comforting place and be still in that place and he will restore our souls. But we're often deceived into coming up with our own plans to restore ourselves that are different than Gods.

People are spirits. They have a soul and live in a body. The soul is the "real you," including personality, likes, dislikes, and tendencies that make everyone unique. We all get off balance sometimes with our thinking. God's word is the solution to being manic-depressive and all other disorders. He will put us back in balance if we allow him.

Doctors practice medicine but can't heal. The human body is designed to heal itself. Psalm 129:14 says we are wonderfully made. If you buy a $100,000 car and something goes wrong, would you take it to a backyard mechanic? Chances are you would take it back where you bought it because they have the most knowledge about the product, its tendencies, parts, how to fix it, and how it was made. They also have a vested interest in standing behind the product because their name is on it. It's the same way with God. He knows everything about us because he designed and made us. He has a considerable amount invested in us- including the life of his only son.

The best cars in the world require maintenance or they'll become run down, get out of alignment, etc. Without routine maintenance, parts will wear prematurely, and they won't perform like they're supposed to. If left without maintenance for too long, even the best car in the world will eventually destroy itself by the motion and wearing of its own parts against each other without proper lubrication. Psalm 23 basically says God will sometimes make us come in for maintenance. When he does, he restores us. For saved people walking in God's will, it's not an option. He makes us do it because he stands behind his products. As his children, we carry his name, and should perform up to a certain level. Maintenance is built into the plan. Medicine can treat symptoms, but God will fix the problem.

The concept of not worrying or being anxious recognizes that I can't fix or help anything. It's a little bit like someone with limited knowledge and computer skills, going to work with Bill Gates and approaching him with a brilliant idea they thought of over the weekend. Or, with the car example, going into a garage to oversee a tune-up or repair, despite not having any mechanical expertise. When I take my car to the shop, I don't have to watch or give my input to have faith that it's getting done right. I believe they know what to do and will perform it. Many times even saved people can impede God's plan if they're not in a position to be quiet, de-stress and listen for direction.

Christians often ask for godly intervention, then later try to fix the very situation they prayed about in their own way. It can be like saying, "OK, thanks God, I'll take it from here," and heading off in the wrong direction. Humans have pride, want to take credit, and wrongly believe they can handle things that they don't know enough about. The reality is that they don't know what they don't even know. It's kind of like playing on a basketball team with Michael Jordan or LeBron James or playing doubles tennis with Serena Williams. The most awesome thing you could do is get whatever direction they have to offer and stay out of their way!

10

YOU HAVE AN ENEMY: HUNT OR BE HUNTED

My fifteen-year-old son recently started wrestling. Though it wasn't a sport I played, I was able to give helpful advice after observing one of his matches. I noticed some things that appeared needed to be successful: (1) if the opponent has you in a bad or submissive position, you must fight to get out! (2) after you escape, or before being put in a bad position, you must attack to put the opponent in a bad/defensive position.

People who have never wrestled or fought probably wouldn't appreciate how grueling and tiring it is. One particularly simple, yet primitive maneuver I observed to be effective was simply pushing the other guy's head down. Satan was an intruder in the Garden of Eden, but Eve allowed him to talk and hang out awhile, not knowing her actions would open the door for her son (Cain) to one day kill her other son (Abel). In Genesis 3:14, God put the devil in an inferior position; "And the Lord God said unto the serpent, Because thou hast done this, thou art cursed above all cattle, and above every beast of the field; upon thy belly shalt thou go, and dust shalt thou eat all the days of thy life." As Christians- agents of Christ in the Earth realm – our job is to keep him where he belongs.

On one day, I observed my son escape a hold his opponent had put him in. After he escaped, he seemed tired and content to stay in a neutral position. His neutral approach posed no threat to the other guy. My son wound up on the bottom again and lost the match to an opponent who wasn't more powerful or better than him, but more aggressive and with a consistent strategy. When he wasn't actively trying to take down or put a move on the opponent—it inevitably led to him being put in a bad position himself. If he got the other guy in an uncomfortable position, he seemed to escape if my son didn't actively try to do something additional.

In a fight with two people or forces going against each other, neutrality has no place. At any time, one of the participants is gaining or losing advantage in their momentum and position. The Holy Spirit and Bible reveal the same thing happens in everyday life. People don't have a chance if they don't realize they're in a fight for their lives and their loved one's lives—both natural (temporary) and spiritual (eternal). If you don't even realize an enemy is actively trying to take you out, you can't properly defend yourself. If you know but react passively, you will lose and wind up in a bad spot not meant for you.

To be successful, we have to be relentless.

John 10:10 says the devil, also known as "the thief," has a simple three-part mission to (1) steal, (2) kill, and (3) destroy. He's never sitting back relaxing. He has no shortage of operatives stationed in hospital rooms and every place you could imagine, working together and carrying out his plans.

Satan is motivated, time conscious, and has tremendous urgency and work ethic. In 1 Peter 5:8, it says he walks about like a roaring lion, seeking whom he may destroy. *The Usual Suspects*, a movie in the mid-90s, accurately depicted satanic tactics when actor Kevin Spacey said the devil's greatest trick was "convincing the world that he didn't exist." It's hard for anyone to defend against something they don't think exists.

Like a serial murderer or burglar, if the devil appeared as himself, few people would let him hang around. Most would be frightened or disturbed and call on Jesus immediately (resulting in Satan's swift departure).

The devil is much more advanced than people. He has thousands of years of historical information and is able to predict the future with some accuracy. He knew our relatives, things they were good at, where they failed, what they died of, and orchestrated many of their deaths before it was time. He knows each person's individual strengths and weaknesses, He's thorough and has dedicated employees who report information to him in detail and carry out his wishes. He knows every person better than they know themselves, including their likes and dislikes.

The Bible says not to give place to the devil (Ephesians 4:27). As mentioned above, if he showed up at our home looking hideous, we'd scream and call on Jesus, which we have the authority to do. But if he can work through the right person—such as someone we find attractive, a trusted family member, etc., —he's often welcomed and embraced. Because he knows how to appeal to emotions and preferences, people are often willing to overlook warning signs that they are dealing with the devil who is a thief, murderer, rapist, etc.

The devil's mission statement in John 10:10 says clearly that he is a thief. Thieves are opportunistic. They rarely retire. They're always looking for the next entry/opportunity. A lion (as Satan is compared to in 1 Peter 5:8), is a hunter; sneaky, dangerous, and opportunistic.

Ephesians 6:12 makes it clear there's a struggle: "For we wrestle not against flesh and blood, but against principalities, against powers, against the rulers of the darkness of this world, against spiritual wickedness in high places." The Bible says the spirit of rebellion is like witchcraft (1 Samuel 15:23). It took me a long time to understand this. But the truth is there are only two things going on in the world when it comes down to it: good and evil. If something contradicts God's word, it's evil. We have to decide and clarify in our own mind which side of the fight we're going to be on.

We've all heard someone say if a person's actions don't hurt anybody, then what they're doing is OK. The problem with that is that they have set themselves up as lord over their own lives, operating on what they see as right without regard for God's authority. The devil loves this and ultimately has his way if they don't repent. They fail to see that they're destroying their lives and harming others (including those close to them). They're lost and don't understand that, in addition to fighting satanic forces, they're in a struggle with their own self. Some don't want to come to terms with being lost because they don't want to change.

In 1 Corinthians 15:31, Paul says, "I die daily," letting us know a struggle is constantly going on. We have to constantly fight with ourselves to live right, because our hearts are wicked (Jeremiah 17:9). Before Adam and Eve ate from the tree of knowledge of good and evil, humans didn't have this problem—all they knew was good. Adam was commanded to have control ("dominion"—Genesis 1:28). The serpent was the most "subtle" animal God made. Satan used it to get close, not to Adam directly, but first to his wife. Because Satan's presence was allowed/entertained, it led to disobedience which caused the suffering and death still going on to this day. In reality, they could've stopped or thrown him out immediately. To avoid Adam's and Eve's mistakes, we can't get comfortable. We must go to war with the devil every day, with ourself and thousands of fallen angels and human operatives working to advance Satan's agenda. Once we understand the constant battle going on, it's clear that we need God's help to stay on track!

Humans tend to be lazy, and the concept of a daily, constant fight can seem like too much, until we realize what's at stake. To appreciate what's at stake we first have to realize who we are, who the devil is, and what he's trying to do. God loves us. The devil hates God, therefore; he hates and is jealous of humans. He resents God's favor, love for us, and our hope for the future because his is doomed.

Even God's angels wonder why he loves us so much (1 Peter 1:12). God made all the beautiful things in the earth for us to enjoy and rule over. Satan wants to destroy us. He wants us to worship him, an inferior being, which will take us out of position and lead to eternal death.

The devil's plan for us, when executed, is like having the son of Bill Gates or Donald Trump living homeless and cut off from their parents with no idea they have access to financial resources. Whenever their dad calls, they don't answer; or when they do talk, they ignore his advice and requests and do their own thing instead.

I tell my children they can take my advice or have a lot of problems they could otherwise avoid. Some people, as the saying goes, have to learn the hard way. What's worse is someone who *never* learns. There is nothing more pitiful than a sixty, seventy, or eighty-year-old fool.

After receiving the Holy Spirit, I finally figured out that rules and boundaries in the Bible aren't to keep me from having fun. They're designed so I can have fun the right and safe way that God intended. They're not designed to make me miserable. Quite the opposite. It's a blueprint to live right and safe and avoid unnecessary pain. Most unsaved people—and some saved as well—reject beneficial messages.

Besides the devil, the man or woman in the mirror is a real and deceptive enemy. In fact, the human heart is more than a little tricky. As mentioned before, Jeremiah 17:9 says it's "deceitful above all things, and desperately wicked…"

Our heart (emotional nature, which includes our mind) often works with the devil to decide against our best interest and cause us to hurt people (including ourselves), forfeit benefits, and generally live beneath our privilege. The reason is that there are a lot of things that aren't good that our body wants to do. Like the analogy of Donald Trump's son being homeless, we all must come to some kind of spiritual awakening to break the pattern of harmful thinking and behavior passed down to us from Adam. We're unable to have this "awakening" on our own. It takes the help of God through his Spirit, ministers, etc. My hope is it will also happen through this book.

Luke 15 tells the story of the prodigal son who moved far from home, wasted all his money partying (on "riotous living"), and wound up living in a pigpen. But he came to himself and realized he had a good family, a good home, and that his father loved him. He realized his dad's servants were living better off than he was because of his bad decisions. He came to himself, realized he didn't have to live that way, and returned home. But how did he start hanging out with pigs? And how did he come to himself? The Lord must help us break through the fog of deception and wrong thinking in our minds. Once God helps us see, we must be willing to change—in this instance, get up and leave the pigpen. Some people don't want to change. They like it and choose to stay. One reason is that they're used to it and think they know what to expect.

God already knows if, when, and how we're going to respond. One of the scariest things that can happen is for God to leave us alone and turn us over completely to our minds. It's scary because Proverbs 14:12 says, "there is a way that seemeth right to a man, but the end thereof are the ways of death." The Amplified Bible version says, "There is a way which seems right to a man and appears straight before him, but its end is the way of death."

11

LOVE

In Matthew 24:12, Jesus's disciples asked him for signs of his second coming. Jesus replied that, in the last days, "because iniquity shall abound, the love of many shall wax cold." (The NLT version says, "Sin will be rampant everywhere, and the love of many will grow cold.")

In Matthew 22:37–39, Jesus said, "… Thou shalt love the Lord thy God with all thy heart, and with all thy soul, and with all thy mind. This is the first and great commandment. And the second is like unto it, Thou shalt love thy neighbour as thyself."

My wife and I were fortunate that around the same time we got married, our pastor began a month's long series talking in detail about what love really is (not just people's idea of it). It's not a sensation or emotion, but more so taking on someone else's burden, challenge, or struggle, wanting the best for them, and being willing to sacrifice your own comfort, food, advantages etc., for them. When there's no love, my comfort and situation is what's important to me. When love is diminished or absent, violence and crime increase.

Of the many things Jesus taught, he said love was the "great" commandment. A commandment is a rule, meaning not a suggestion, but a requirement to follow Jesus correctly. Therefore, for anyone who claims to be Christian (meaning "Christ-like"), love should be their priority. Love doesn't come easy for humans. A baby, after all, wants what they want and quickly learns how to obtain it. They love their mother automatically because they're close to her and she's a source of great comfort, food and life itself. Neighbors tend to be more focused on themselves. Many are nasty and self-centered, but Jesus said to love them anyway, as much as we love ourselves. This isn't an easy directive to carry out. It's so difficult, almost no human can do it consistently. Because Jesus knew that, he sent his Holy Spirit in his absence to replace and over-ride the sin nature we received from Adam. "But the Helper, the Holy Spirit whom the Father will send in My name, He will teach you all things, and remind you of all that I said to you" (John 14:26, NASB).

When we let God cultivate love in our hearts through Jesus, the need for other commandments is minimized. When we operate from a position of love toward others with the help of the Holy Spirit, we won't hurt or kill them; steal from them, we won't be jealous of their possessions or success, try to take their spouse, etc. When we love ourselves more than others, harmful activities abound. Because human hearts (minds) are deceitful, they're masterful at making up excuses to justify bad activities.

When crime and offenses go up, they increase animosity and desire for revenge, which causes a vicious circle where satanic activity thrives and feeds off of itself. It's easy to see it operating in neighborhoods, families, workplaces, etc. Christians, with the help of the Holy Spirit, are "salt" and "light" put in place to expose and change these cycles. Their counterculture, love, and approach expose evil (which is easy to see as the norm) and change the flavor of situations. "Ye are the salt of the earth: but if the salt have lost his savour, wherewith shall it be salted? It is thenceforth good for nothing, but to be cast out, and to be trodden under foot of men. Ye are the light of the world. A city that is set on a hill cannot be hid." (Matthew 5:13–14).

God's will is for people to live in harmony and peace. John 13:34 says, "A new commandment I give unto you, That ye love one another; as I have loved you, that ye also love one another." This is the underlying foundation for all the previous extensive rules and laws. The New Testament is like a new, simplified deal where our obligation is to love God and our neighbors—easy to remember, right?

It's impossible to operate in love consistently, without assistance. Jesus knew this better than anyone. This is one reason he made the gift of the Holy Spirit available. In John 16:7 NLT, Jesus said, "But in fact, it is best for you that I go away, because if I don't, the Advocate won't come. If I do go away, then I will send him to you."

Human emotions are unpredictable. Based on what's going on, we can feel drastically different from day to day or even minute to minute. With God's spirit inside us, we can act based on God's ability instead of our own. For instance, with our natural mind, we might see a person who seems hateful and unapproachable for no reason. The Holy Spirit knows additional facts: they could be struggling with unbearable loss, trying to recover from abuse, etc. The Holy Spirit knows secret facts. The truth is, if we lived through the same things some others have, we'd be much worse than them or might have given up all together.

Through the Holy Spirit, we have the power to help people consistently and change situations for the better. We can stand out as examples of how humans are supposed to treat each other. In Matthew 5:15–16 (NLT) Jesus said, "No one lights a lamp and then puts it under a basket. Instead, a lamp is placed on a stand, where it gives light to everyone in the house. In the same way, let your good deeds shine out for all to see, so that everyone will praise your heavenly Father." Even when operating out of concern for others, without the Holy Spirit, we'll make mistakes that can cause more harm than good.

In a suburban community where we lived, an upper middle-class family took in a troubled teenager with a drug addiction to live with them. He was an athlete with great potential. It might have seemed like he just needed some stability. It seemed like a great idea. Unfortunately, after taking the young man in, their own child began using hard drugs and, tragically, passed away from an overdose. This is one reason it's so important to have and be led by the Holy Spirit. The Bible provides general and specific wisdom and truth, while the Holy Spirit provides daily personalized guidance, education and protection in real time. All of this being said, I won't assume those parents weren't led by the Holy Spirit. I don't have all the information and can't judge that situation – besides, that's not my job.

As a Christian, my job (currently) isn't to judge, but to tell and demonstrate the Gospel (good news) and what it looks like to live a holy life. The good news is that when we love God, we can do good consistently because God knows everything before it happens, and he accounts for our mistakes. As mentioned earlier, Romans 8:28 says: "And we know that all things work together for good to them that love God, to them who are the called according to his purpose." This is an awesome statement directed specifically toward those who love God. What does it look like to love God? This is set forth in John 14:15, where Jesus said, "If ye love me, keep my commandments."

As humans we can keep God's commandments, be kind and make right decisions. But we can't be totally consistent. The Holy Spirit opens up a whole new world inside of us where we can act consistently and be quick to repent when we fall short. It keeps us positioned to be "salt" and "light."

As mentioned before, there's ultimately only two things happening— life, love, and obedience on one side and fear, disobedience, and death are on the other. The Holy Spirit helps us stay on the right side of the equation and return quickly whenever we go astray.

12

SATAN: PRINCE OF A CRUMBLING SYSTEM

God doesn't change. His plan from the beginning is the same plan today. Genesis 1 shows God's plan.

The earth was a custom-made, all-inclusive paradise for humans to rule over and worship God. Genesis 1:27–28 (NLT) says, "So God created human beings in his own image. In the image of God he created them; male and female he created them. Then God blessed them and said, 'Be fruitful and multiply. Fill the earth and govern it. Reign over the fish in the sea, the birds in the sky, and all the animals that scurry along the ground.'" The King James Version says, "have dominion over the fish of the sea, and over the fowl of the air, and over every living thing that moveth upon the earth." Webster's online dictionary defines "dominion" as "sovereign or supreme authority; the power of governing and controlling." Adam was one man commissioned to be the navy, army, and air force!

Luke 10 says, "And he said unto them, I beheld Satan as lightning fall from heaven." So, to summarize; God created the Earth and put Adam in charge. Satan was thrown out of heaven and landed on Earth. He was an outcast with no power who used operatives to get to Adam and convince him to give up his authority.

Because he's smart and cunning and doesn't bring anything good, Ephesians 4:27 says, "Neither give place to the devil." In Genesis 3, when Satan appeared through the snake, lied, and contradicted what God said, Adam had authority to throw him out. His choice to allow him to stay and to entertain the lie he'd told Eve led to Adam's disobedience, though he was supposed to be the leader. This led to Adam being cast out. God's rules and commands are given to help and protect us, often against things we can't see. Disobedience to God has many built-in consequences that don't just stop with one generation. One man's disobedience to God (sin), opened all humans up to evil and death. Evil spirits do evil things. They aren't stagnant, but very driven and constantly work to advance evil agenda. As a result, they're still running rampant and moving into new areas today—thousands of years later.

In our society, it's easy to be desensitized to the word "evil." A few specific examples are school killings, mass shootings, rape and robbery. If Adam hadn't sinned there would be none of this. There would be no hospitals or intensive care units. Sin opened the door for all of these. When we see these things in proper perspective, we can hate evil like God does.

As stated before, Peter 5:8, says "your adversary the devil, as a roaring lion, walketh about, seeking whom he *may* devour." Use of the word "may" suggests he can't just devour anyone, but basically needs permission.

Not only have lax humans who aren't on their jobs allowed evil, they often celebrate it. When I visited New York City, there were framed pictures of The Notorious B.I.G. (who rapped about robbing a pregnant woman, raping children and throwing them over a bridge) hanging in several establishments like he was a great person who benefitted society. If society not only allows but glorifies sin, including rape, robbery, and murder, there are consequences the people will live with.

A common false belief I've seen play out many times is that evil can

CHRIS HARRIS

be permitted and contained from spreading. Decades ago, I witnessed people in small towns talk about drug abuse dismissively as a "city" problem. Today, addiction and overdoses ravish those same small communities. The reason is that evil spirits move around and call their friends to come over (Matthew 12:43-45 and Luke 11:24). They're always looking for new entrances and people to use. By the time people trying to live without guidance of the Holy Spirit realize there's a problem, it's often too late. Pain, grief, and suffering can multiply and go on for generations. Some things can lay dormant, skip some and affect later generations. The carnage unleashed in the garden of Eden is still happening today. Though Jesus gave humans the power to stop it, most people won't because they don't realize what's going on, don't know how to fight spiritually, or don't want to because they enjoy aspects of sin they don't want to give up (you can't be involved in sin and effectively fight against it at the same time). The good news is that the evil system allowed to be put in place is crumbling and won't go on indefinitely. Many Bible scholars predict it will end soon.

Genesis 1:1–2 (NIV), the first passage in the Bible, says, "In the beginning God created the heavens and the earth. Now the earth was formless and empty, darkness was over the surface of the deep, and the Spirit of God was hovering over the waters." For whatever reason, the earth was covered with darkness and water until God decided to bring light, trees, etc., and populate it with people.

The apostle John wrote Revelation (last book of the Bible) while exiled on an island. Revelation 21:1–4 (NIV) says, "Then I saw 'a new heaven and a new earth,' for the first heaven and the first earth had passed away, and there was no longer any sea. I saw the Holy City, the new Jerusalem, coming down out of heaven from God, prepared as a bride beautifully dressed for her husband. And I heard a loud voice from the throne saying, 'Look! God's dwelling place is now among the people, and he will dwell with them. They will be his people, and God himself will be with them and be their God. He will wipe every tear from their eyes. There will be no more death or mourning or crying or pain, for the old order of things has passed away.'" This lets us know God is coming to remodel the Earth completely and clean up and correct what people let be destroyed. For those truly against and tired of the pain and suffering that accompanies sin, this is great news! But those who hold on to sin will stay separated from God eternally. It wouldn't make sense for them to have access to the new heaven and earth—they'd simply let the devil in to start the cycle of pain, suffering and death all over again.

In Joshua 24:15 (NIV), Joshua gave the tribes of Israel a summary of their family history before telling them, "But if serving the LORD seems undesirable to you, then choose for yourselves this day whom you will serve, whether the gods your ancestors served beyond the Euphrates, or the gods of the Amorites, in whose land you are living. But as for me and my household, we will serve the LORD."

For anyone reading these words, I make the same appeal to you that Joshua made thousands of years ago. Be intentional. Be wise. Don't wait. Choose this day who you will serve.

Printed in the United States
by Baker & Taylor Publisher Services